Dedicated to my grandchildren,
Joshua and Hannah Laidler,
Josey Lawrenson and any future additions!

Posy Tales

by

Lorna Laidler

Additional illustrations by
Joshua Laidler and Hannah Laidler
With thanks to Sarah Tai.

Contents

Photographs

Front:
Small Boy viewing the Small Islands from Smirisary, Inverness-shire

Contents Page:
Wild Irises and Foxgloves overlooking Eigg and Rhum from Samalaman, Inverness-shire

Back:
Wild Flower meadow Howick Hall, Northumberland

Printed in Great Britain by L & S Printers
Camperdown, Tyne & Wear
Tel: 0191 216 1717

Dandelion

Dandy the lion gazed round, he was bored,
He lived in a lion park owned by a Lord.
It was all very nice he was watered and fed,

He had several fine wives and a comfortable bed.

But Dandy was jealous, I'm sorry to say
Of the beautiful jackets milord wore each day.
He strutted about, every day his coat new,
Sometimes in yellow and sometimes in blue.

Dandy was sad his own coat to compare
The same every time he looked, just old gold hair,
His mane was quite wispy, his claws rather dull,

His teeth without shine and his figure too full.

His wives sometimes sniggered when Dandy walked by
Or examined their claws or gazed up at the sky,
His keeper did try to make Dandy look good,

He brushed him, had vitamins put in his food.

But Dandy one day had a better idea
And added a flower to the back of each ear.
A spray of green leaves he then pinned to his chest,

Determined of all lions he'd be the best

His wives and his children lay under a tree
So Dandy pranced by saying, "just look at me,"
His tail stuck out straight and his head held up high
With a spring in his step and a gleam in his eye.

His ladies stared at him in sheer disbelief,
They laughed at his flowers and his spray of leaf.
His children first sniggered, then giggled and roared
To see their old dad try to copy a Lord.

That night in the lion house his family slept,
But Dandy, awake lay and silently wept.
Of all the wild beasts, lions should be the king
And here he was such a sad tatty old thing.

Suddenly Dandy smelt burning and smoke,
He roared at his family until they awoke,
He roared once again with a ferocious shout,His
keeper rushed over to let them all out.

The flames from a cigarette carelessly thrown
Had started a fire which had quietly grown,
His family trembled and whimpered with fear,
Dandy ran to them, his duty was clear.

Between the flames quickly he ushered them out
Then turned as behind him he heard a shrill shout.
Back in the corner behind all the flames
His tiniest cub stood there calling his name.

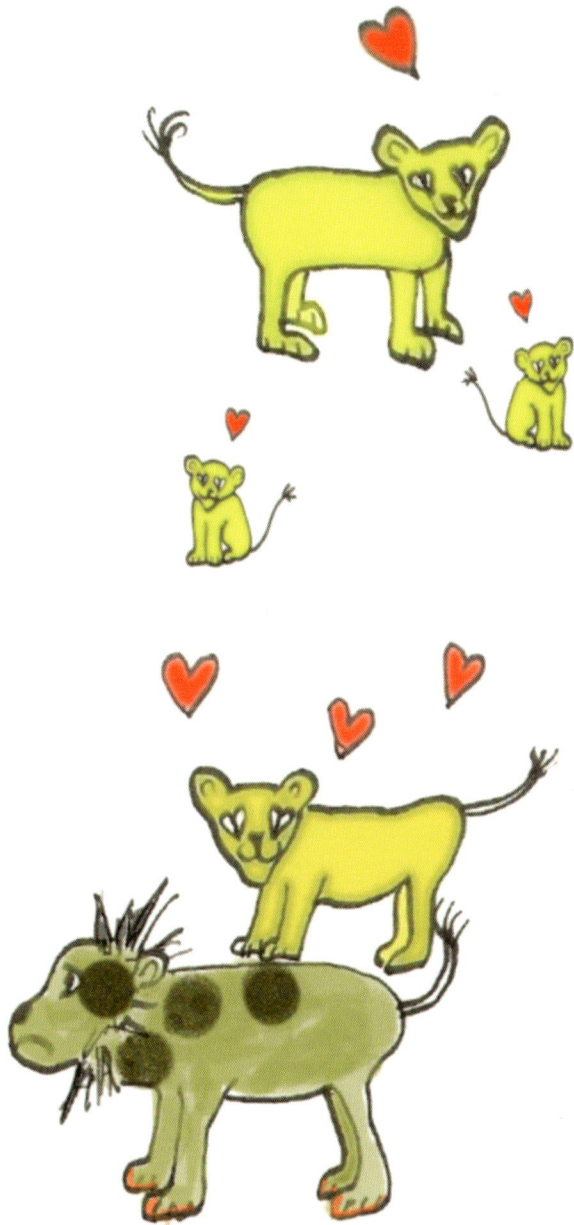

Without hesitation he leapt through the fire
And to his cub's side Dandy ran to stand by her.
She gazed at her father, her eyes full of tears
But Dandy with confidence said, "have no fears".

Gripping her firmly he ran through the heat
Ignoring the burns on his mane and his feet,
Safely he dropped the cub back with her mum,
The rest of the pride stared at him, quite dumb.

Dandy looked down at his singed ruined coat,
A tear in his eye and a lump in his throat.
He never could ever look kingly again
With a smokey singed coat and a wispy burnt mane.

His wives were regarding him quite dewy eyed,
Their gaze filled with love, adoration and pride.
His children all boasted their dad was so brave
He'd saved them from fire and a premature grave.

The lionesses kissed him on each blistered paw,
Milord stuck a medal on old Dandy's door,
His children made garlands of flowers of gold.
"Dandelions" they said as they crowned him I'm told.

All children know the dandelion's fluffy seed head, the
"Globe of down
The schoolboy's clock in every town."
Some children know the dandelion as 'piddley bed'
because of its habit of leaking a white fluid from the
leaf, stem and flower when picked.
Its traditional meaning is more dignified :- Happiness,
Devotion.
The name 'Dandelion is actually a corruption of the
French 'dent de lion', the tooth of the Lion because

of the jagged shaped leaves.

Daisy

"Look out girls, here comes the mower,
We'll all have to keep our heads down."
"Has he set the cutting blade lower?"

One daisy asked with a frown.

The lawn mower swept through among them,
The blades were set thankfully high,
Some lost the tips of their petals, but then

Some lost their heads and would die.

"Thank goodness I'm still here", one daisy
Said with relief to the sky
Me too, but my sister was lazy

She didn't duck, so its goodbye!

The name Daisy comes from 'Day's Eye' because of the flowers
habit of of opening with the daylight.
'This earliest playmate of the little ones', used to be known
inNorthumberland as 'Bairnwort'. The name seems
to have fallen out of use but the daisy is still beloved of small
children far and wide as they weave them into daisy chains.

This tiny flower has a strong connection to the name 'Margaret',
being the emblem of two Saint Margarets (of Antioch and Cortona).
Hence one of its old names, Saint Margaret's herb.

It was also the 'device' of Margaret Tudor, mother of Henry 7th
and Margaret of Anjou, wife of Henry 6th.

In France it was the emblem of Marguerite, sister of Francis 1st.

William Wordsworth wrote of the daisy,
'Small service is true service while it lasts,
Of friends, however humble, scorn not one.
The daisy, by the shadow that it casts
Protects the lingering dew drops from the sun.'

The flower meaning of the daisy , as befits a flower beloved by
Children, is 'innocence'.

Dog Rose

A skinny dog named Rose
With a black and shiny nose
Was loitering outside a butchers shop,
Her brown eyes open wide
Gazed at butcher boy inside
In case he dropped a sausage or a chop.

On his bike the boy set out
To distribute meat about
To his customers both in and out of town.
Rose tucked herself behind
Thoughts of food upon her mind,
As she followed him up every street and down.

At last Rose seized her chance
When without a backward glance
Dan the butcher boy left his bike unattended.
From its basket sausage links
Disappeared in a blink,
Rose's rumbling little tum would soon be mended.

Dragging sausage Rosie ran,
Out of sight of butcher Dan,
Round a corner safe, she started on her feast.
Tucking into sausage meat,
Never heard the sound of feet,
Until Dan said, "You're a hungry little beast."

"Come back to the shop with me
You shall have some beef for tea,
And a juicy bone to chew on through the night."
Rose has landed on her feet,
She has all she wants to eat,
As the butcher's dog she really does alright.

Dog Rose was so named because dogs were said to eat the hips.
An abundance of rose hips in the autumn is said to foretell
a hard winter. Rose hips are an important source of food
for birds and were made into tarts and conserves in Elizabethan
times. After the Second World War school children were
encouraged, by being paid 3 old pennies, (about 1p) per pound, to
gather rose hips and bring them to school where they were collected
to make rose hip syrup, an important source of vitamin 'C'
in those days when food was still rationed.
The story goes that all the first roses created were white, but one
grew on a long slender stem and stretched over to see her reflection
in a nearby stream. On seeing how beautiful she was, she blushed
pink and became the mother of all roses.

The flower meaning is 'Purity'.

Forget-me-Not
(The legend of how she got her name)

After the creation
The Lord had to decide
On names for all the flowers He'd made,
So time was set aside.

The largest and the brightest
Were named and listed first.
The smallest had to wait their turn,
Some with impatience burst.

One tiny flower was worried,
Her petals white and small
The Lord might simply overlook
And never see at all.

She summoned all her courage
And gave a little shout,
"Dear Lord oh please forget me not."
Then shrank back, tired out.

Would her dear Lord be angry?
Or worse, not even hear?
But He'd noticed her distress
And gently He drew near.

Her white and dainty petals
He touched and turned to blue
"Just like the heaven above," He said
"A clear and azure hue."

"And as for what to call you
Why, we shall use your prayer
You will be called 'Forget me Not'
Oh flower both sweet and fair."

Another, more tragic, story of how the Forget me Not came
by its name springs from Germany.
It is the tale of a young Knight, who, having returned safely
from the wars, was walking by a stream with his lady love
telling her of his many adventures. She drew his attention
to a pretty blue flower growing close to the water's edge. He
stooped to pick some, then plunged into the water to reach
the best specimens. The bank was steep and slippery, the
current was strong and as the river washed him away he threw
the blue flowers up to his lady love , calling "Forget me not."
The flower meaning of the forget-me-not is 'true love'.

Fox Gloves

You are cordially invited to attend,
You may even be accompanied by a friend,
The dress required is formal,
For a hunt ball this is normal,
The handwritten Invitation kindly said.

Freya Fox was so excited to be asked.
To find a dress would be a pleasant task,
A rich purple would be nice
Was her mother's sage advice
Though her own taste ran to rich and ruby red.

To celebrate the end of hunting season
Each year the ball held for that very reason,
It had taken place for years,
But now midst many tears
The hunt ball as an event would soon be dead.

For hunting would be coming to an end
Freya'd heard the news from Freddie Fox, her friend,
So this last ball must be good,
There'd be dancing, drink and food
And a lot of fun before 'twas time for bed.

Freya

Freddie

Freya searched through every clothes shop for a dress,
Some looked OK, others frankly looked a mess.
Then she found one that was right
That she'd wear for the big night,
It was purple (matching feathers for her head)

All the other foxy ladies who were going
Had been shopping, or in some instances sewing.
Bags and shoes had been acquired
So that they would be admired
When by partners to the dance floor they were led.

When the morning of the ball finally dawned,
Freya rose from bed and daintily she yawned,
She laid out her dress and shoes,
Thought which evening bag she'd choose,
When a discomforting thought entered her head.

There was something that her outfit was without.
Evening gloves were lacking still, there was no doubt.
It was Sunday, shops were closed,
A real problem now was posed,
Freya's heart was filled with worry and with dread.

She did not want to be a laughing stock
In her dancing shoes and lovely purple frock,
But without gloves to compare
With the feathers in her hair
She'd just have to stay at home and go to bed.

"Oh dear mother" Freya cried in some distress,
"I've no gloves to match the colour of my dress!"
"Do not worry daughter dear,
There are gloves aplenty near,
I wore a pair of them when I was wed".

Freya's mother stepped outside into the wood
Where some purple flowers elegantly stood,
Plucking two flowers from the stem,
Handing Freya both of them,
"One for each front paw my dear" her mother said.

To the hunt ball Freya finally set out,
Partner Freddie whirled and twirled her all about.
Lots of fun was had by all
At the final Fox Hunt Ball,
They have picnics every weekend now instead.

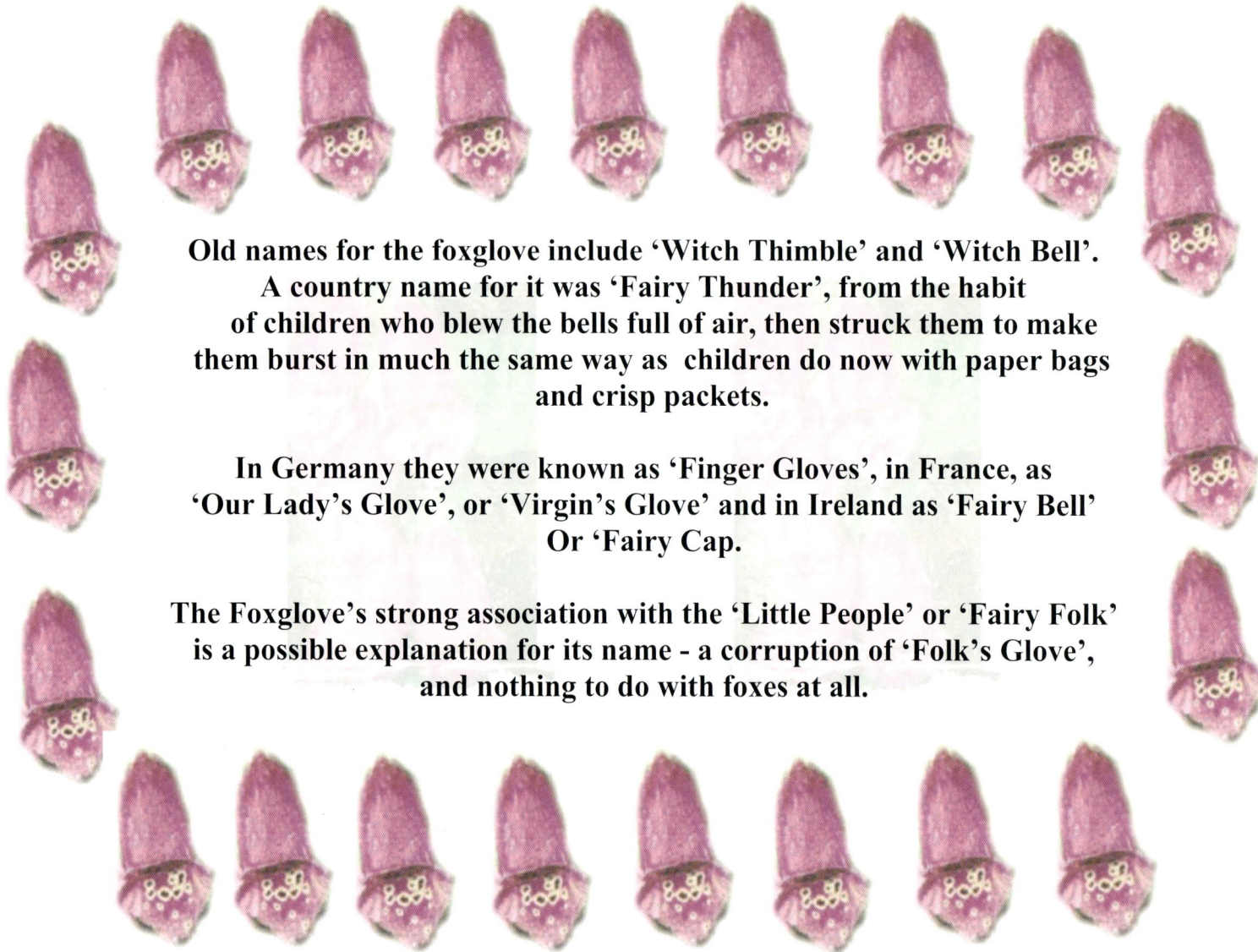

Old names for the foxglove include 'Witch Thimble' and 'Witch Bell'.
A country name for it was 'Fairy Thunder', from the habit
of children who blew the bells full of air, then struck them to make
them burst in much the same way as children do now with paper bags
and crisp packets.

In Germany they were known as 'Finger Gloves', in France, as
'Our Lady's Glove', or 'Virgin's Glove' and in Ireland as 'Fairy Bell'
Or 'Fairy Cap.

The Foxglove's strong association with the 'Little People' or 'Fairy Folk'
is a possible explanation for its name - a corruption of 'Folk's Glove',
and nothing to do with foxes at all.

Thrift

Mrs. Blackbird took care of her pennies,
Never spent two when one would have done.
Her nest was constructed of what came to hand
But neatly and skilfully spun.

She shopped with an eye for a bargain
And allowed not a morsel of waste,
Her chicks cleared their plates without fail 'cause
All their meals had a wonderful taste.

The family's clothes were all home made,
But carefully laundered and pressed.
No children who lived in the woodland
Were ever more beautifully dressed.

No bounty that came ever squandered,
No good opportunity missed,
The chicks were all taught by their mother
The habit, and value of thrift.

And so, when the nest they were leaving
Out into the world for to fly,
They all had a wonderful nest egg
From the savings their mother put by.

Thrift is also known as the Sea Pink or
Sea Turf owing to it's habit of growing on cliffs
and near the sea shore.
The flower meaning is 'sympathy'.

Primrose

"ROSE!" The shout would echo
Through garden, house and street,
"Tidy yourself up my girl
Your sister is so neat."

But Rose's jeans were grubby,
Her hair was such a mess,
Her wellies mud bespattered,
She wouldn't wear a dress.

Her finger nails were dirty,
Her neck circled with grime,
Her mouth was always chewing gum,
Her bedroom was a crime.

Her poor mother was frantic
To see her daughter so.
Her other girl, a picture,
But Rose, a picture? NO!

Until, that is, new neighbours
Moved into number one.
They had a red Mercedes
And a rather dishy son.

Rosie smartened up her act,
Her wellies got the boot,
She brushed her hair, put on a dress
And sandals on each foot.

Rose became quite friendly
With young Jim at number one.
The neighbours were amazed to see
The girl she had become.

The change in Rose was stunning
Once she'd encountered Jim,
From looking such a total mess
Rose was now quite prim.

In times gone by the lovely primrose was
chosen to strew before the feet of rural
brides and carried in her bridesmaid's bouquets
to express good wishes and hopes for
future happiness.
The flower meaning of the primrose is 'Early Youth',
or 'I need you'.

Pussy Willow

Willow the kitten, with fur of dove grey
Opened green eyes to a sunny spring day.
Out through the cat flap in search of some fun,
Over the garden she went at a run.

Once in the wood she looked back at the house,
When she came home perhaps she'd chase a mouse.
But now she was off to find what she could
Out in the depths of the dark leafy wood.

First was a frog that she loved to make jump,
A rabbit she chased into a bramble clump.
Then a strange flower that flew in the sky,
(She learned when much older, its name, butterfly)

Finally sleepy, curled up on a log,
Dreams were soon shattered by sounds of a dog.
Ears pricked upright, green eyes open wide
Willow looked quickly for somewhere to hide.

Under the log she went huddled up small,
When along came a puppy dog chasing a ball.
Pink tongue out hanging and long waggy tail,
Poor Willow's courage was starting to fail.

But snuffling and sniffing the puppy dog came,
"Hello there young pussy cat, tell me your name."
Out flashed a paw and the claw of a cat
"Ow!" cried the puppy. "Why did you do that?"

"You gave me a scare." Willow hissed in reply
"What are you doing here, with whom and why?"
"I'm here with my owners; we're out for a stroll
And then I caught sight of you tucked in this hole

My owners are good kids, no trouble at all
I keep control of them by using this ball.
As long as I bring it and get them to throw,
I persuade them to follow wherever I go."

"My name is Willow and no one owns me,
But I do live with people, on that I agree.
They feed me and stroke me and I share their home
But I'm free as I can be to wander and roam."

"You're Willow!" The puppy dog said with a start,
"My children are looking for you, cross my heart.
They came to these woods to find something for school,
It's called Pussy Willow, it's found near the pool.

You are a pussy, and Willow's your name
So maybe to find you is the reason they came"
"You soppy dog," Willow said, flicking her ear,
"Pussy Willow's a tree that grows just around here.

Come and I'll show you now, just follow me
Right by the pool, do you see that small tree?
There are many small furry grey catkins on that,
But they'll never grow into a beautiful cat."

Pussy Willow

Pussy Willow (or Goat Willow) is only one of
many types of Willow tree. The bark of the
White Willow has been used for centuries as a pain
killer and in the 19th century, a form of Asprin was
first produced from it.
The wood of the Willow is also used to make
cricket bats.

Ragged Robin

"What a disgrace!" The young robins all said
With their jackets of brown and their waistcoats of red.
Behind every wing they went twitter and tweet,
With their shiny black eyes and their feathers so neat.

The bird that they spoke of and gossiped about
Was scruffy, with some of his feathers pulled out.
He'd arrived in the wood just the previous week,
With colours so dull and a twist in his beak.

"We think he's a robin". They said with a frown,
"But his red is all dusty and look at his brown!"
The sad little bird said, "I've had an escape
From a cat with long claws and a mouth all agape."

"He was after my family just out of the nest,
So I pecked him, in spite of the fear in my breast."
"You pecked at a cat!", the birds said in surprise,
"Perhaps our opinion we'll have to revise.

No wonder your feathers and beak are a mess,
From you ragged appearance no one could have guessed
That you are a hero, a robin of note."
At that our friend robin just opened his throat.

The tune that he warbled was thrilling and clear,
The listening robins all gave a loud cheer,
The birds of the woodland admired his song,
The notes were so pure and he held them so long.

"Your beak may be twisted, your feathers astray,
But please, in our wood may we ask you to stay?
If you teach us your song so that it becomes ours
We will bring you, our hero, a tribute of flowers."

This lovely summer flower is usually (but not always) found
growing in damp ground. Other names it has been
known by include 'Torn Coat', Flower of the Cuckoo',
'Robinet' and 'Bachelor's Buttons' because of the
ragged cloth buttons commonly worn by old bachelors
in bygone days.
It is closely related to and resembles that other summer
flower, 'Red Campion'.

Ragged Robin

Red Campion

The Cowslip

Rebecca sat day dreaming
Beside a quiet stream,
With yellow cowslips growing round,
How beautiful they seemed.

A herd of cows stood grazing
Upon the grass nearby,
A picture of contentment
Under the summer sky.

Rebecca looked from flower to cows,
"I wonder how it came
That pretty yellow flower
Has such a funny name."

"Rebecca, it's like this my dear,"
Said Mirabell the cow,
"Listen very carefully
And I'll explain right now."

My great great great great grandma
Once jumped over the moon
And on returning back to earth,
She came home pretty soon."

"Looking for a nice cool drink
To this stream she returned,
She stretched her neck to reach
Then with embarrassment she burned.

"My great grandma slipped down the bank
To end up cross and wet,
"I slipped" she gasped, "how can that be
To a high flying cow like me?"

"Something must have tripped me,
Just wait till I find out."
She looked for someone else to blame
And gave an angry shout!

"There's the one at fault" she cried,
"That flower is to blame,
I must have slipped on it so
Now Cowslip can be its name."

Rebecca smiled at Mirabelle
"That makes the whole thing clear,
Thank you for your story."
"Don't mention it my dear."

This Springtime relative of the Primrose was known by the name of 'Paigle' in southern England. Believed to be beloved by Fairies, it was also known as 'Fairy Cups', 'Fairy Keys' and 'Fairy Clusters'.
Alternatively, it was sometimes called 'St. Peter's Wort', 'St. Peter's Keys' or 'Springwort'.
An ointment of Cowslip leaves was used to remove freckles or tan from the skin.

Giant Hogweed's Wedding

There was a young giant named Hogweed
Who was looking around for a wife,
His eye had been caught by sweet Violet,
She'd make a good partner for life.

Sweet Violet lived in the valley
Helping grandma to care for her farm,
Grandma Lily kept cows sheep and horses
And chickens and ducks by the swarm.

Mint, the cat loved to doze in the garden,
Flax the toad lived there under the hedge,
While Parsley, the cow chewed the cud in the field,
Grandma Lily grew flowers and veg.

One morning the household awakened
To a terrible banging and crash.
Lily quickly donned her ladies mantle
And Violet her smock with a dash.

Into view at the end of the valley,
Giant Hogweed strode over the land.
"Lily of the valley I'm coming
To ask for your grand daughter's hand."

Sweet Violet was quite astonished
Her eyes out on stalks with surprise
"I don't even reach to your kneecaps!
I can't even look in your eyes!"

"I've borrowed a ladder from Jacob"
Said Hogweed with disarming smile,
"Climb up and you'll see I'm so friendly,
Just stay and we'll chat for a while."

Sweet Violet was quite charmed by Hogweed
But the animals weren't very pleased,
The sheep ran and hid in the sorrel
The duck and the chick, they both weed!

The Bull rushed around in his paddock
And stood on the little colt's foot,
The mare flicked her tail in annoyance
And said he was a clumsy brute.

Then blowing a blast on his bugle
Hogweed called "I have something to say
Forget me not, I'll be back shortly
Sweet Violet has named the day."

Jacob's Ladder

"We'll deck out the farm for the wedding
With beautiful bright yellow flags.
There'll be singing and dancing and feasting
And everyone wear their glad rags."

"But first to the church we will hasten
Before we sit down to the meal,
To celebrate Vi and my wedding
And seal it with Solomon's seal."

The wedding day came very quickly,
Violet's bridesmaid, young Poppy, wore red.
The folk showered Vi with rose petals
"A beautiful bride," they all said

The couple were happily settled,
The family followed quite fast.
The first to be born were Hazel and Fern
With Heather and Hyacinth last.

There are twenty five plants in this story,
In each verse you will find flower names.
Can you find them? (Would you recognise them?)
In your garden or down country lanes.

Plants in the poem 'Giant Hogweed's Wedding'

(The names of all these plants are on Page 36)

9

10

11

12

13

14

15

16

17

18

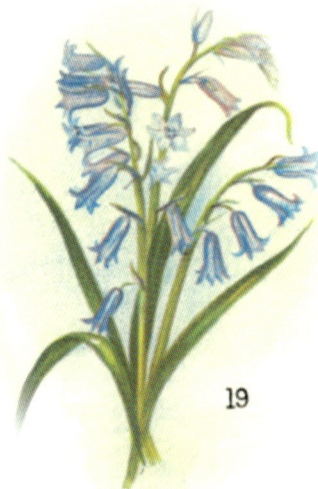

19

20

21

22

23

24

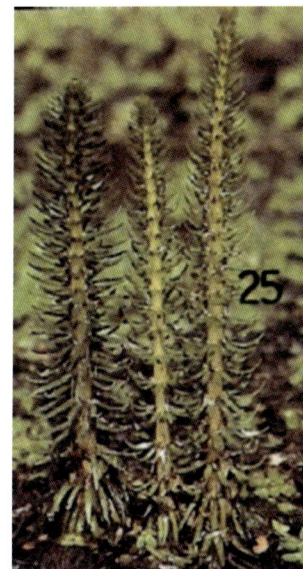

25

List of Plants in the poem 'Giant Hogweed's Wedding'

(Where known the flower meaning known it is given underneath the name)

Giant Hogweed---9

Sweet Violet---17

(Modesty, Virtue, Contentment and Truth)

Lily of the Valley---22

(Humility)

Cat Mint---1

Toad Flax---13

Cow Parsley---24

Ladies Mantle---15

Ladies Smock---8

Jacob's Ladder---16

Sheep's Sorrel---20

(Affection)

Duck Weed---4

Chick Weed---14

Bullrush---6

Coltsfoot---7

Mares Tail---25

Bugle---2

Forget me Not---12

(True Love)

Yellow Flag (Iris)---23

(Friendship, Message)

Solomon's Seal---18

Poppy---5

(Silence)

Rose---21
(Purity)
Hazel---3
(Reconciliation)
Fern---11
(Sympathy)
Heather---10
(Solitude)
Hyacinth (Bluebell)---19

(Humility)

Also by the same author, 'Up The Valley' and 'Down The Town'.

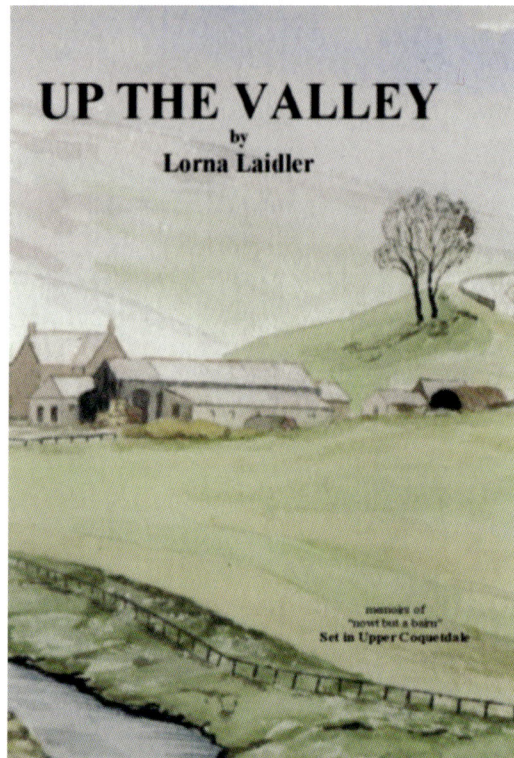

Set in Northumberland's Upper Coquetdale in the late 1940's and early 1950's, a collection of stories and childhood memories of summers spent on the isolated farms in England's most northerly and sparsely populated county. A humorous look, in prose and verse, at a way of life that has now disappeared. Illustrated with line drawings and old photographs.

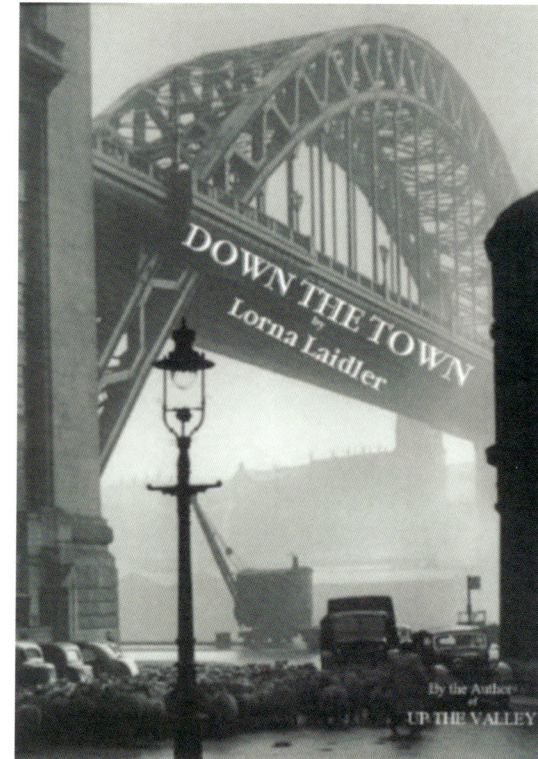

In the differing worlds of town and country, I Have always had a foot in each camp. 'Up The Valley' told of childhood summers spent in Coquetdale. This companion book is the other side of the coin - a policeman's daughter's childhood spent in the streets around Newcastle In the post war years, when entertainment was, of necessity, home made and P.C. Still stood for 'Police Constable'. Tales, humorous and otherwise as the family moved from a 'prefab' in South Shields , then various police houses in Newburn, Seaton Burn and Wideopen, up to the point when they left the town and moved to Wooler at the foot of the Cheviot Hills.